Congratulations on your graduation from ScaleUP! Here's to finding more fabulous...

Sara

FINDING FABULOUS

FINDING FABULOUS

SARA NOBLE

PRINCIPAL PHOTOGRAPHY
BY LAURIE KILGORE

Copyright © 2018 by Sara Noble

All Rights Reserved. No part of this book may be reproduced in any manner without written permission except in the case of brief quotations included in critical articles and reviews. For information, please contact the author.

Cover and graphic design by Novella Brandhouse.

Front and back end sheet prints are Marguerite Embroidery in Sky courtesy of Schumacher.

SARANOBLEDESIGNS.COM

ACKNOWLEDGMENTS

I have a lot of people to thank and this may be my "Oscar Night Acceptance Speech" chance, so to my team who has worked beyond expectations to grow and make Noble Designs the firm it is today: Jessica Gordon, Rachel Clement, Jeanie Scott, Amanda Gooding, Maureen Lindstrom, Ruth Barton, Marianne Mayer and Molly Kovarik – thank you.

To Christina Wendling who pushed me to finish this book and made me sound smart.

To Novella Brandhouse who somehow got in my head and made the pages look exactly how I imagined (or better). And to Laurie Kilgore who tirelessly, and with a smile, took many, many photos for me.

To my parents who were not only always so happy (although often too surprised) at my success but who also gave me my first $5000 to start Noble Designs – I love you.

To my kids, who most of the time, worked with me to accommodate clients by being quiet or waiting for me to go or whatever else they could tell you they sacrificed – I am forever grateful that you are my children. The only thing I am more proud of than my design work is each of you, and the fact that you are kind people I want to be around makes me so happy.

To my best friends, Nikki, Kam, Jen, and Krista who always believed I would not have to go back to a finance job. And to Vince, who taught me to dream big.

PROFESSIONAL ACKNOWLEDGMENTS

Editor Christina Wendling - True Life Legacies
Graphic Design - Novella Brandhouse - www.novellabrandhouse.com
Photography Formaphoto by Laurie Kilgore - www.formafotophotography.com
Additional shots provided by:
Chrissy Wichman
Jamie Borgman
Aaron Leimkuehler - Kansas City Spaces
Roy Inman - www.royinmanphotos.com
Matt Kocourek - www.mattkocourek.com
Alea Lovely - www.alealovely.com
Classic Tressie - www.classictressie.com

CONTENTS

FOREWORD 9
BY TAMARA DAY

INTRODUCTION 11
FINDING FABULOUS

EAST COAST MEETS PALM BEACH 13
THE JUNGER HOME

CASUAL GLAM 39
THE VALENTINE HOME

BOLD COLOR 61
THE SPROTT / MAXWELL HOME

CLASSIC DETAILS 83
THE KELLY HOME

HIPSTER TASTE 103
THE MIGNERON HOME

RUSTIC + MODERN 119
THE MCNALLY HOME

ATTENTION TO DETAIL 133
THE ROSE HOME

EMPTY NEST HIGH RISE 161
THE PENCE HOME

TRADITIONAL RE-FRESH 179
THE THORNBERRY HOME

MY TOUGHEST CLIENT 189
MY HOME

FOREWORD

BY TAMARA DAY

DIY and HGTV host of Bargain Mansions

I met Sara in the summer of 2008 while I was in the midst of the biggest and most personal renovation of my career – my own Bargain Mansion. Sara was working as a designer in a local designer tile and plumbing shop, and whenever I needed a little escape, I would go into the shop and daydream about all the fabulousness inside. Sara was always so gracious and generous with her time. She would often chime in with her thoughts and it was quickly apparent that she had a talented eye. I was just getting my feet wet with higher-end design projects, and I was definitely still on my stay-at-home-mom budget! Sara helped me hone in on exactly what I loved but could also afford.

When I was remodeling my own kitchen, the Tuscan vibe was at the peak of its popularity. I was pushing back against the trend and had big plans of a spacious, white kitchen filled with open shelving. I had at least a dozen people tell me I was crazy, but Sara came over out of the goodness of her heart and encouraged me. She thought my ideas were incredible. I went for it and never looked back.

Sara continued her design business and I started my business restoring vintage furniture. There have been many parallels in our careers over the years, despite moving in different directions. Sara has always been someone I follow, as her sense of style is always on point and her knowledge of business has helped launch her to the next level as a designer. Over the years, I've called on her keen eye more than once to help make the tough decisions in my own home. Every designer needs a designer friend, right?

INTRODUCTION

My mother dragged me to countless antique stores as a child, and although I complained, I think it was there that my appreciation for home design took root. While my mom taught me design, my dad taught me business. My first plan was to be CEO of a Fortune 500 company. I would dress up in heels, get out his old business law books, and play office. Looking back, I feel like everyone should have been worried; strange kid. Anyway, I followed that "Plan A," earned a finance degree, and landed several subsequent jobs that I hated until starting Noble Designs, which finally allowed me to marry my creative side with my business side. It began slowly, as I had small children and truly only worked part-time, but as my kids became more independent and I had more time, my business grew. I was lucky to have on the job training in design and construction along the way. I poured myself into the design world and am proud of the results.

Recently, someone asked me why I was writing a book. Good question, right? The answer should have rolled right off my tongue. After all, I have put much thought and great effort into creating it, but there I was, faced with that question, completely unable to articulate my "why." Despite every life coach's warning that my process was backwards, I forged ahead with the book, and I can honestly say that now, as I review my work, I am sure of my "why."

So, why did I write this book? I did it for a number of reasons. My initial motivation was to share my work. I'm proud of what Noble Designs does and selfishly, I wanted to show it off. I envisioned a beautiful coffee table book to showcase my designs and to serve as a constant reminder of my success. After all, don't most of us need to be reminded that we've done good work? I was also hopeful that this book would serve as a reminder for my clients to use me again (wink, wink!) or to refer me to friends.

That was my starting place, but as I sent each chapter to my various clients for review, I was hit smack dab in the face with the REAL reason why this book is important to me. What I really desire to share with everyone who reads it is this – humanity is good! I have amazing clients with whom I have forged lifelong friendships, and I want to share that side of design, the human side, the connection that gives it all meaning. My clients and I have laughed, cried, and shared life moments together. THAT is what truly makes my job a dream, so I tried, with my ninth grade writing class long behind me, to share the moments that are special and entertaining to me, while also sharing our design vision. I then sent each chapter to the respective client and waited for their approval. Each one not only agreed but shared words of encouragement and kindness that again meant the world to me. For me to accumulate this into my first book is invigorating.

I am inspired by fashion, especially Kate Spade and Jenna Lyons. I adore Dara Caponigro and her eye to make anything she touches beautiful. I could look at images of Jackie Kennedy Onassis for hours. I am drawn to art museums where I find lots of pieces I don't always understand, but then I find the pieces that speak to me and influence my colors and design. While I love the world of social media, I do miss turning the actual pages of magazines like Traditional Home and House Beautiful where I would pull out pages that inspired me (I can't actually give up the hard copies, so those favorites I still pull pages). I think it's important to be daring and personal in design. That's what makes something fabulous – originality and authenticity. After sixteen years of working hard at design, I want to share some of my favorite tidbits, tricks, and tools. Enjoy the beautiful imagery, and I hope you find something fabulous!

SARA NOBLE

INSPIRED BY

classic prep with an adventurous twist

EAST COAST MEETS PALM SPRINGS

THE JUNGER HOME

THIS WAS A DREAM PROJECT — A LARGE REMODEL IN MISSION HILLS, KANSAS FOR KURT AND ELLEN JUNGER, A COUPLE WITH A UNIQUE DESIGN AESTHETIC. FOR LACK OF A BETTER TERM, I CALL IT "EAST COAST CLASSIC MEETS BRIGHT PALM SPRINGS COLOR." MY HEART BE STILL! MUCH TO MY SATISFACTION, THIS PROJECT TURNED OUT NOT TO DISAPPOINT.

Ellen came to me by referral from one of her co-workers, and as soon as she walked into the barn to meet with me for the first time, I knew I was going to love working with her. She has a classic, preppy, old-school, formal style that is somehow fresh and modern. During our pleasant conversation that day, I discovered she grew up wearing Jack Rogers shoes. What could be better?

She is a corporate marketing goddess. It renews my faith in corporate America to see a woman clearly able to lead with authority, but who can also succeed while demonstrating compassion. I rarely name drop other clients just in case there's a conflict, but I have used Ellen's name to my advantage countless times because there is not a soul who doesn't like her. Thanks, Ellen!

Kurt, her husband, is another example of what we hope for in mankind. He is a smart, capable man and a great, stay at home dad. He is decisive, kind, and non-judgmental, which is a strange yet refreshing combination.

Together, they have given me much. Kurt provided insider information on the driver's education program I enrolled my son in, and Ellen modeled for me the power of going for the job you want. They led me to one of my favorite re-upholstery businesses, and their general contractor, John Noblit, was such a joy to work with that we cemented a lasting working relationship. The Jungers and I also share the struggle of having bright children who need a little pushing. Sorry kids. We're certain you will thank us later, or at least we cross our fingers and hope.

No project of this size is without its hiccups, and the Junger home was no exception. The master tub was a tight fit, the first living room rug was awful, and when Fiona's bathtub drained, it sounded like a tornado barreling through her bathroom. In the end, everything turned out beautifully. The design gods must've been trying to tell us something with that first rug because the second one we tried was absolutely meant to be in the space, and it turned out that an $11 drain cover fixed the problem in Fiona's bathtub. Ellen and Kurt remained calm and always kind as we tackled these and other issues, which is one of the reasons they are some of my favorite people. It is always appreciated when clients realize that this isn't brain surgery, and we can work on solutions together that will make everyone happy.

They don't know it yet, but I enjoy their company so much that I intend to be their friend. Watch out Jungers, I'm your new friend, but on a happy note, I do come with wine.

SARA'S TIPS
FOR
EAST COAST MEETS
PALM SPRINGS

Color is our friend. Embrace it and use it in your decor.

Bold drapes in bright colors make me happy. Find what makes you happy and use it!

It doesn't hurt to have a father that is an artist. If you have it, hang it up! The rest of us are jealous.

If you have a big room, think about splitting it into two areas. This great room got fireside seating and guest seating with two sofas and chairs. The two areas created in this one space fill it up visually and serves multiple purposes. Don't forget the dry bar.

Pink is not just for girls. Blush adds warmth to a space. Use it with confidence everywhere.

INSPIRED BY
luxury on the lake

CASUAL GLAM

THE VALENTINE HOME

SEVEN YEARS AGO, WHEN I FIRST BEGAN WORKING WITH CAYLEE VALENTINE, NEITHER OF US WOULD'VE EVER IMAGINED THE LASTING FRIENDSHIP WE WOULD FORGE. SHE HAS BEEN A PIVOTAL CLIENT FOR MY BUSINESS AND AN IMPORTANT CONFIDANT IN MY LIFE.

Caylee sought my help to create a design plan for her twin daughters who were thirteen at the time. They each had their own rooms with a shared bath and loft in the upstairs of their home, and it was time for a refresh. Although the girls are identical, they have vastly different interests, tastes, and preferences, which allowed me to explore my inner girl for two completely different styles – the ballerina and the field hockey player. It was so much fun! It was also one of the first times a client said, "Do it!" in response to my proposal – no edits. We implemented the room designs exactly as I envisioned them. To have the complete trust of the family in that way meant a great deal to me, both then and now.

I am proud that the rooms reflect each girl's unique personality, and that both spaces are beautiful and timeless. One of my greatest compliments came just recently when we photographed the rest of the home and everyone thought the girls' rooms looked as if they had just been completed. It is awesome to think that a project completed seven years ago can still be relevant. A testament to fresh design based in classic elements

Far beyond being a fabulous client, Caylee is a friend and inspiration. I look forward to my visits out at the lake. We've been on too many diets to count. She always wins. Whatever she is doing is apparently working, while my diet of peppermint candy cane blizzards and Manhattans is not paying off as well. Besides sharing our little struggles in life, she has helped me through a divorce, coached me on how to help my son who struggled with reading, and continues to talk me down when teenage girl drama seems overwhelming. Caylee's daughters are three years older than my Ellie, so her experience and honesty have been invaluable to me. She talked me through the oh-so important theatrics of Homecoming, first boyfriends, and college Rush which is looming in the future for our household. Her advice is solid and thoughtful. This former teacher and small-town girl has her head on straight and constantly inspires me to be a better mother, girlfriend, and woman.

So, to Caylee, I say a heartfelt thank you. You have impacted my life for the better. You and your family will always hold a special place in my heart. Your kindness, generosity, and beauty are evident and appreciated.

And to the reader, I hope you're as inspired as I am by the beautiful pictures of this beautiful home.

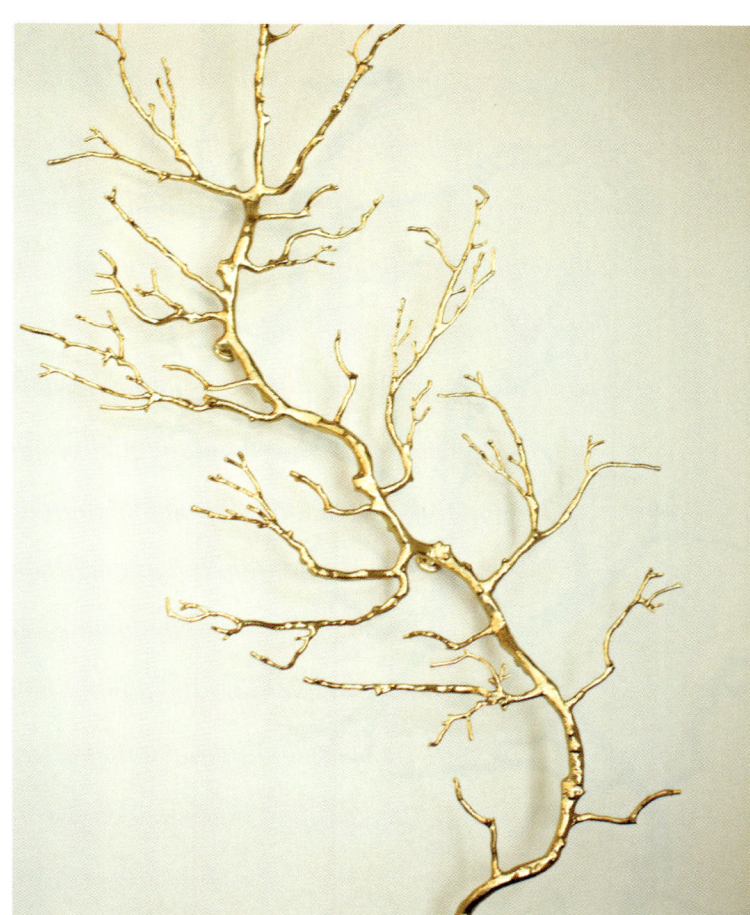

52

SARA'S TIPS
FOR CASUAL GLAM

Take a rustic element, like reclaimed wood on the wall, and then contrast it with a modern element like brass sconces. The mix of the two makes it interesting.

Wallpaper an accent wall. We wallpapered bed walls in the master and both girls' rooms. The paper made it personal and dramatic. We used a black paper in the master that may have seemed too much for the entire room but on the bed wall it's the perfect pop to offset the upholstered bed.

Build an infinity pool with a hot tub on your lakefront property. Of course.

Throw a cow hide down as a rug to bring in casual glam. Turns out cows don't stain so the durability is a plus.

BOLD COLOR

THE SPROTT / MAXWELL HOME

THOUGHTFUL, BUT DARING DESIGN — THAT IS HOW I WOULD DESCRIBE THE AMAZING MISSION HILLS, KANSAS HOME OF RYAN SPROTT AND MOLLY MAXWELL. I WAS BROUGHT IN DURING THE CONSTRUCTION PHASE OF THIS TOTAL GUT JOB PLUS ADDITION, A JOB THAT WAS A TRUE UNDERTAKING AND COULD'VE BEEN QUITE A HEADACHE BUT TURNED OUT TO BE A REAL JOY.

With three small boys in tow, the youngest being only two at the time, Ryan and Molly tackled this renovation head on, making the most of the space while still respecting the traditional Tudor style architecture of the home. They kept much of the original wood trim, moldings, and ceiling lines, but with little hesitation, agreed to wallpaper ceilings, install bold, modern lighting, and utilize unexpected paint colors and graphic fabrics. They are one of the only clients I've ever worked with who readily agreed to my favorite "blowfish" wallpaper in their powder room, and perhaps the most interesting feature of their remodel is a full-sized basketball court in their basement. That's right – full sized!

I made a few daring choices of my own, some of which required me to do a little persuading. In the kids' wing of the home, I talked Molly into painting the lower half of the entire area black, including the framing around the windows and doors. Understandably, they were a little apprehensive about it at first, but I persisted. Now, if I'm being honest, it IS scary to push a client into something because if they don't end up liking it, I feel completely responsible. In this case, however, we were all pleased with the dramatic results. When it's a happy ending for all, that is beyond exciting for me and one of the best things about my job.

One of my favorite rooms in this house is the game room, a small, traditional space that we updated with dramatic drapes and bold fabric on the chairs. Ryan and Molly possess an amazing art collection which allowed us to create beautiful gallery walls in this room, and we chose to keep the original floor, a calico stone tile — incredibly unique and undoubtedly interesting.

I often develop girl crushes on my clients, and Molly, who is smart and unassuming, is no exception. I adored her from the start. I could tell by the way she dressed that she had impeccable taste, which I loved, but more importantly, I watched the way she interacted with people and liked her even more. Everyone with whom she comes in contact receives genuine kindness, and it's what makes her one of my favorite people.

I will be forever grateful to Ryan and Molly for their friendship and excellent referral which led to many more projects in Mission Hills. Plus, if I ever want to get in a little game of basketball, I know where to go!

SARA'S TIPS
FOR
BOLD COLOR

One of my favorite tricks of the trade – bold lighting. It's an easy way to give a space a facelift and a fresh, modern feel.

Using black paint is an inexpensive way to add depth, dimension, and drama. Although this was a new choice for me on this project, it has now become one of MY tricks of the trade.

In keeping with the more traditional style of architecture, we kept the classic frames of much of the furniture but reupholstered them in bold, graphic prints to add interest.

We reused many things from the original house. The basement bar table was an old wooden door that we lacquered red and attached legs to, creating a fun, modern, upcycled piece of usable art.

In the guest suite addition, we reused drapes from elsewhere in the house but gave them a more modern feel by painting the ceiling a glossy blue and adding bright red side lamps for a punch of color.

INSPIRED BY
blue & white southern charm

CLASSIC DETAILS

THE KELLY HOME

I FIRST MET MOLLIE KELLY WHILE REDECORATING THE CLUBHOUSES OF SOME OF THE APARTMENT BUILDINGS SHE OWNS WITH HER HUSBAND, PAT. I ENJOYED WORKING WITH HER SO MUCH THAT IT WAS A PLEASANT AND WELCOME SURPRISE WHEN THEY GUTTED THE FIRST FLOOR OF THEIR PERSONAL HOME AND ASKED ME TO BE THEIR DESIGNER.

Mollie is truly a designer in her own right, so I was thrilled to collaborate with her on this large project that we tackled right before the wedding of their only daughter.

While working on the clubhouse designs, I had gotten to know Mollie's taste in style, which is admittedly more traditional than my own, but I looked forward to working with more classic elements and adding modern details and finishing touches. And that is exactly what we did. Mollie is the queen of details. If there's trim or fringe to be had, we used it, and the results were beautiful. One example is a chair we recovered in a gorgeous Ralph Lauren plaid, which would've been amazing on its own, but we finished it off with a touch of fringe around the edge of the seat cushion. Timeless, classic, tasteful, and fun.

My two favorite spaces in the Kelly's home are the master bathroom and the dining room. The master bath, with gleaming white marble is like walking into Carrara heaven. Stunning. The navy-blue walls in the dining room are striking, but the buffalo check navy and white drapes steal the show. The drapes were out of Mollie's comfort zone initially, but once she saw the dramatic effect they created, she was on board.

I also had to persist a little bit to convince them to paint the master bedroom blush. Most people worry that any shade of pink will be too feminine, but the addition of darker, more masculine wood pieces created a balanced master retreat.

Independent and strong, Mollie is a role model for me in many ways. We had to be careful during our design meetings as we could quickly veer off course and talk for way too long about our personal lives. She possesses a well-defined sense of style and knows exactly what she wants and what she likes. When you see her, she is always put together in a classic but up to date way that makes you wish you had her closet.

Pat and Mollie are truly amazing people, both individually and as a couple. They run their business the way I aspire to run mine, treating every single person with the utmost respect, from the designer to the tile-layers to the floor-cleaners. Likewise, they treat one another with enormous respect and care. They always greeted each other with a kiss, Mollie always took Pat's calls, even if she was in the middle of craziness, and he always responded so kindly to her requests. Their kids, Laura and Ben, are just as gracious as their parents. They were truly a joy to work with and a pleasure to be around.

SARA'S TIPS
FOR
CLASSIC DETAILS

Add trim to unexpected spaces. Mollie has always added fringe to cushions, giving them a rich finished look.

Do not skimp on the drapes. Windows framed out by beautiful drapes make a huge statement. Do not go cheap on these, darling. You'll regret it. It's eye level and catches people's attention.

Use a full rod. The drapes are just panels adorning the sides of a window or bank of windows, but they should look like they could work – use the long rod.

Add modern touches to a traditional space. The Lucite coffee table is a perfect example of modern meets classic.

INSPIRED BY

modern, artistic aesthetic

HIPSTER TASTE

THE MIGNERON HOME

ONE OF THE MOST UNEXPECTED, YET PLEASANT SURPRISES ABOUT BILL AND KATHY MIGNERON IS THEIR MODERN DESIGN AESTHETIC. ALTHOUGH THEY ARE GRANDPARENTS LIVING IN A TRADITIONAL RANCH STYLE HOME IN MISSION HILLS, THEY ARE FAR FROM WHAT ONE MIGHT THINK OF AS TRADITIONAL OR GRANDPARENTS. THEIR HIP STYLE, LOVE OF ART AND TRAVEL, AND FEARLESSNESS WHEN IT COMES TO NEW IDEAS MADE THEM SO EASY TO WORK WITH AND SO MUCH FUN.

Our working relationship began when they wanted to refinish their fireplace, but it quickly grew from there, one project at a time. Together, we tackled a massive outdoor remodel, making the most of their spacious, beautiful lot and the canopy of Mission Hills trees in their backyard. The outdoor living space now features great hardscapes, a patio with a built-in grill, a modern firebox, sectional seating, and giant umbrella to shade it all. Kathy even placed a full-sized dining room table outside, making it the perfect spot for entertaining.

We were able to do a lot, making the best use of what we had when it came to their master suite. The Migneron's master bathroom is on the small side, but typical for a home of that age and style. That didn't stop us from making it spectacular, though. The bathroom boasts heated towel bars and modern underlighting beneath the tub. Kathy was always open to suggestions and up for anything new and different. The kitchen retained its original layout but got a fresh coat of paint on the cabinets, beautiful monotone quartz countertops, and a stunning black marble backsplash. Their piano room is a testament to the fact that just a little bit can go a long way to reinvigorate a space. We added fresh paint, a new rug, and new artwork on the walls, and "Voila!" It looks like a brand-new room.

I introduced Kathy to a local artist I love, Cali Hobgood, and just as I had hoped, Kathy fell in love, too. She purchased several of her pieces to highlight throughout the home in addition to the impressive art collection they already owned. Kathy has impeccable taste and naturally mixes art and textiles that have a more global vibe with more classic elements to create a truly eclectic feel.

I often describe my clients as kind and caring, but when I say that about the Mignerons, it is at a whole different level. I was working with them on their master bed/bath remodel the first year after my divorce. That Thanksgiving was going to be the first holiday I would not get to spend with my children. It came up in conversation one day while we were meeting with the contractor, and without skipping a beat, Kathy invited me to eat Thanksgiving dinner with them. I have family in Kansas City, so I had plans and was well taken care of, but Kathy's genuine hospitality struck me and stuck with me.

The very first to order from my online store, Kathy and Bill have turned out to be some of my biggest supporters, and for that, I am extremely grateful. Their dedication to their family, their generous hearts, and their modern style make them FABULOUS in my book.

SARA'S TIPS
FOR HIPSTER TASTE

Don't be afraid to grab real estate wherever you can get it. In the guest room, we transformed a closet into a special jewel box work area.

Cali Hobgood is a favorite artist of mine whose work I was able to share with the Mignerons. Using a collection of her work in the master bathroom provided a high end feel to this newly renovated space.

Find pieces that speak to you. Kathy found a pillow on Etsy that featured fabric designed by artist, Hunt Slonem. The chic bunnies add an artistic touch even to the sofa.

Grab a drink, enjoy a beautiful patio in lovely Mission Hills, and take in the Plaza Art Fair flags hung for outdoor art!

RUSTIC
+
MODERN
=
DREAM
HOME

THE MCNALLY HOME

AMY MCNALLY AND I GO WAY BACK, AND I DO MEAN WAY. WE'VE BEEN FRIENDS SINCE CHEERING TOGETHER IN HIGH SCHOOL AND WENT ON TO BE COLLEGE ROOMMATES. SINCE THEN, I HAVE WATCHED HER CREATE A BEAUTIFUL LIFE FOR HERSELF AND HER FAMILY ALONGSIDE HER LOVELY HUSBAND, ED. HAVING THE OPPORTUNITY TO WORK WITH THEM TO CREATE THEIR DREAM HOME WAS TRULY AN HONOR AND A PRIVILEGE.

Ed and Amy's project was a new build on a picturesque piece of acreage. Ed is an avid hunter, so they wanted something cozy, like a country cabin, but something that still felt modern and functional, like a family home. We blended rustic and modern elements in subtle ways to create a homey, practical, and comfortable space for the entire family. We carried the natural stone on the fireplace all the way up to the ceiling but flanked it on either side with beautifully crafted, refined cabinetry, giving just a little nod to that lodge feel without being too literal.

As the project got underway, it quickly became apparent that Ed and I have similar, "fancier" tastes than Amy, so there were several times when we had to join forces to talk her into various design elements. One of those was the beautiful marble countertops in the kitchen. Amy's practical side worried about something happening to them. By convincing her that marble is forever and forever classic, Ed was able to win her over. She also needed some persuading about the fantastic light fixtures we chose for the kitchen. She thought they looked like fishing bobbers… and in all honesty, once she pointed that out, they kind of do.

Amy quickly agreed to black windows, which really set off the view. The light walls are a great backdrop to the country outside. We added sconces above the kitchen windows which was the perfect finishing touch. With good bones the extra decoration is just a perk.

My friendship with Amy has grown sweeter and deeper over the years. I will be forever grateful for her love and support during my divorce. Amy and I were college roommates but were on opposite schedules. I was an early to bed early to rise and Amy was the exact opposite. While I'm guessing neither one of us completely "got" the other I enjoyed her different and relaxed outtake on life. Amy worked in the corporate world for many years before doing what we all felt was her calling. She went to hair academy and opened her own salon. Another testament to karma working to bring her great things as she brings so many great things to others.

Perhaps the greatest thing about designing a friend's home is that I get to visit and enjoy the fruits of our combined labors. Thank you, Amy and Ed, for your friendship and fun and the opportunity to make your home a special place for you and your family for years to come.

SARA'S TIPS
FOR
RUSTIC + MODERN

Create contrast. High contrast draws your eye to those elements. Black windows and light walls allow the window frames to pop, and with the scenic land surrounding this beautiful home, we want you to notice the view.

Add light fixtures. We installed two light fixtures in this dining room, fitting the scale of the room perfectly. One large light fixture often gets too wide and creates a hazard when standing up from a rectangular table. This option allows us to keep the size appropriate for over the table but address the length of the table and the room.

Create an interesting powder room. You don't need expansive storage in this room despite what mom might say. You need toilet paper and not much more, so have fun with this room and do something unexpected rather than the traditional vanity.

Don't forget it's hard to have a mudroom that's too big. Build in closed storage. No one wants to see your clutter. Pretend you live like this and shove everything behind closed doors. No one will be the wiser.

Carefully recreate your high school cheerleading dance to fully embarrass the kids. When you can do it in a pair, it adds extra delight to the performance. Perhaps skip the toe touch jumps so no one gets hurt.

INSPIRED BY

details that deliver

ATTENTION TO DETAIL

THE ROSE HOME

AMY HAWLEY ROSE IS LIKE NO OTHER CLIENT I HAVE EVER WORKED WITH, AND I MEAN THAT AS A COMPLIMENT. A FORMER KANSAS CITY NEWSCASTER, SHE THINKS LIKE A JOURNALIST, ASKING THOROUGH, THOUGHT-PROVOKING QUESTIONS AND GATHERING ALL THE ANSWERS BEFORE MAKING A DECISION. SHE APPROACHED THE REMODEL OF THEIR FAIRWAY, KANSAS CHARMER IN MUCH THE SAME WAY, WHICH MEANT THAT EVERY DETAIL WAS WELL RESEARCHED, PLANNED AND THOUGHT OUT. THE END RESULT WAS, OF COURSE — FABULOUS!

Amy left her job as a newscaster to be home with her four young children. I was constantly amazed at her ability to be present to them while at the same time, tackling this extensive renovation. She is the supreme multi-tasker. We met weekly and went on various fun field trips to find precisely what Amy wanted. I think we literally visited every showroom in town to look at every slab of marble. We also spent hours in Kansas City Building Supply, perusing door and cabinet handles. I loved every minute of it!

Amy invested their money in good pieces but saved her money when she could by doing her homework and taking her time. She purchased an amazing La Cornue stove from Williams Sonoma but saved money by finding a matching vent hood on eBay. She worked tirelessly on creating custom metal doors for the front pantry in the kitchen. It was no easy task as we had to design the perfect door and then make it fit the budget.

The house has many notable features, one being the marvelous black inlay in the wood floors in the entry way. The floors throughout are actually original – we just stripped them down and lightly stained them so that all the original wood grain shows through.

The mudroom is practical and beautiful with its dark green lockers, cabinetry, and desk. The entire house got new windows, extensive interior trim work, and the white oak vanities in the master bathroom are stunning.

When I think about what makes Amy "fabulous," one word comes to mind – lipstick. Amy always wears lipstick and always has it at the ready. In her kitchen, we designed a small flip-out under the sink where most people might store sponges. Not Amy. She flipped it down to show me one of her favorite ktichen features and there was lipstick – you never know when you might need to reapply. Every woman needs a lipstick cubby built in to her kitchen. I know I do now.

I learn something or gain something new from each and every client. Besides learning how crucial lipstick is, I learned from Amy that persistence for details is always important. Her hard work on the "small things" added to one big beautiful home. I also loved her work style. A woman that asks questions with authority and unapologetically is something to enjoy. I miss her and hope they start a basement project soon.

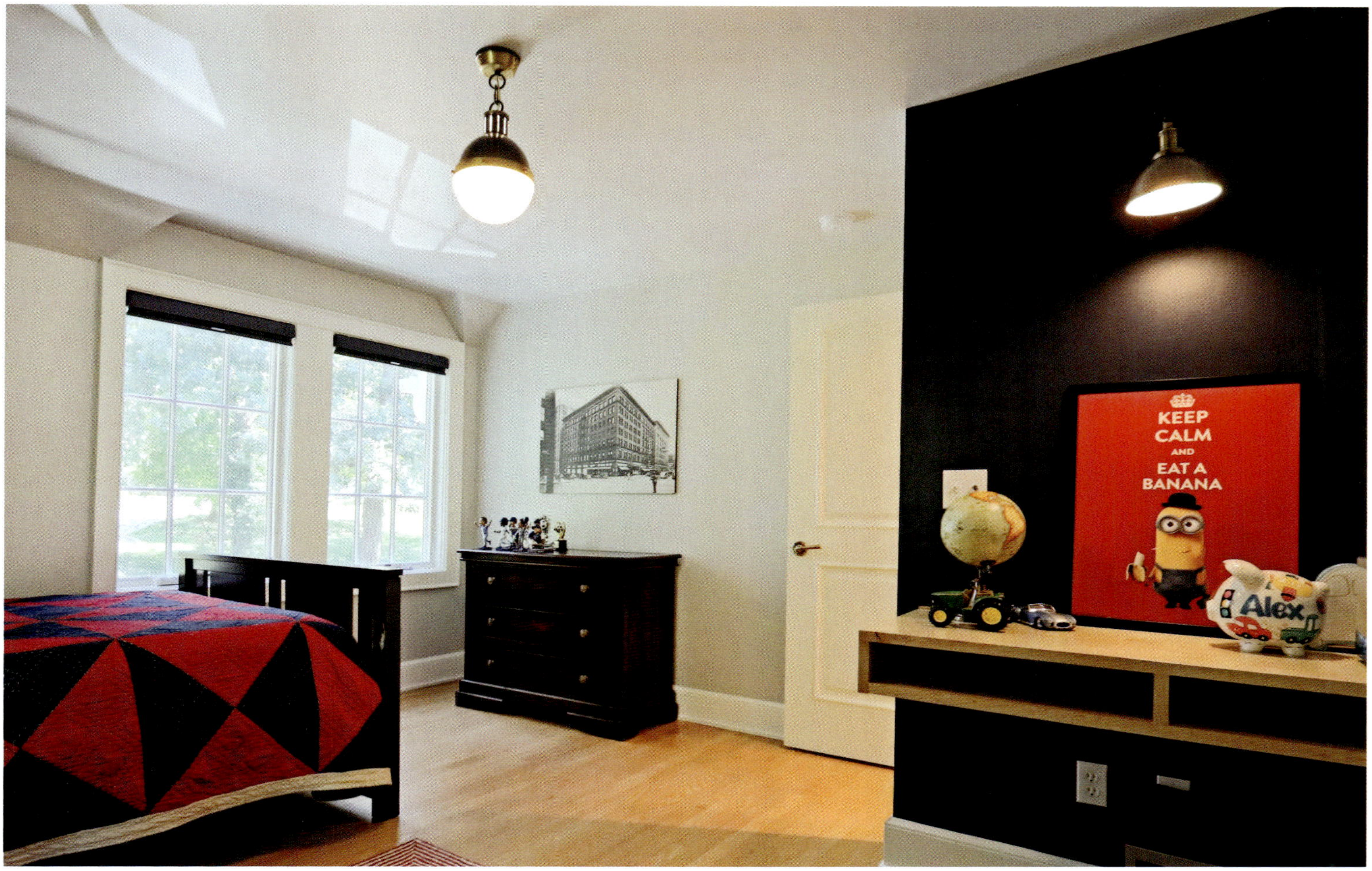
KEEP
CALM
AND
EAT A
BANANA
Alex

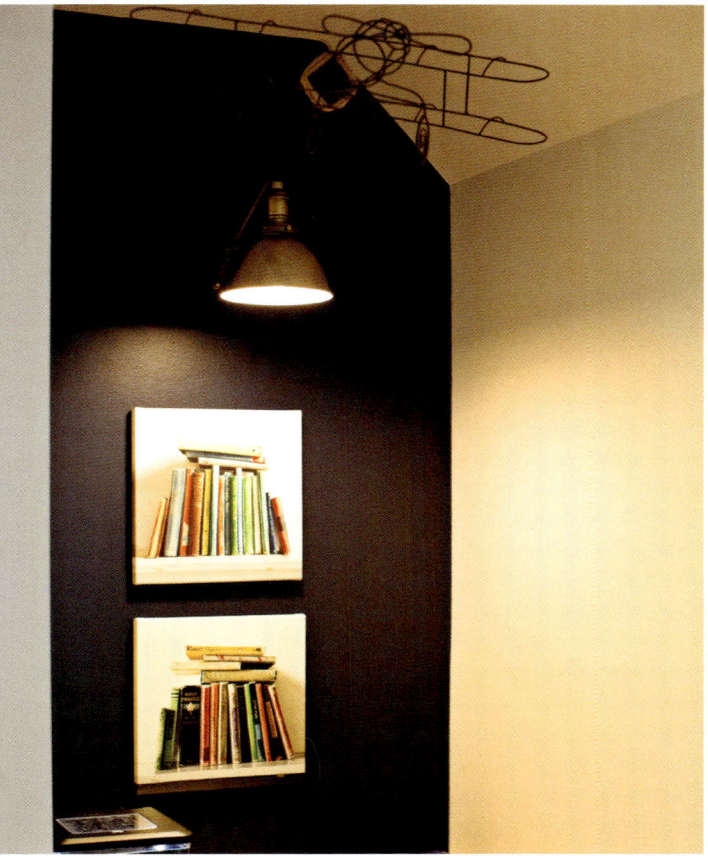

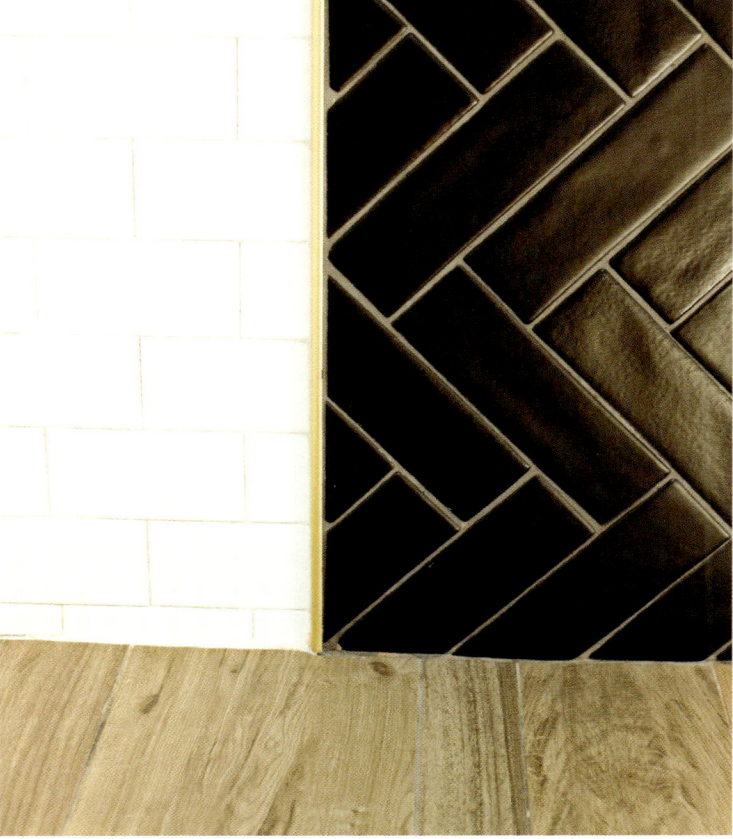

SARA'S TIPS
FOR ATTENTION TO DETAIL

Don't be afraid to mix styles. This bipolar kitchen showcases traditional cabinetry with a modern island. It's unexpected and fun.

Brass rules. I would like to turn everything gold. When we had the chance to add brass details to the built-in dining room buffet, I said, "Heavens to Betsy, yes!"

A pop of strong color goes a long way. The girls' bathroom was mostly white until we hung the hot pink sconces. They woke up the whole space!

Get a La Cornue stove! It's gorgeous, plus Amy reports that it cooks well, too. Bonus!

INSPIRED BY

world travels & an artist soul

EMPTY NEST HIGH RISE

THE PENCE HOME

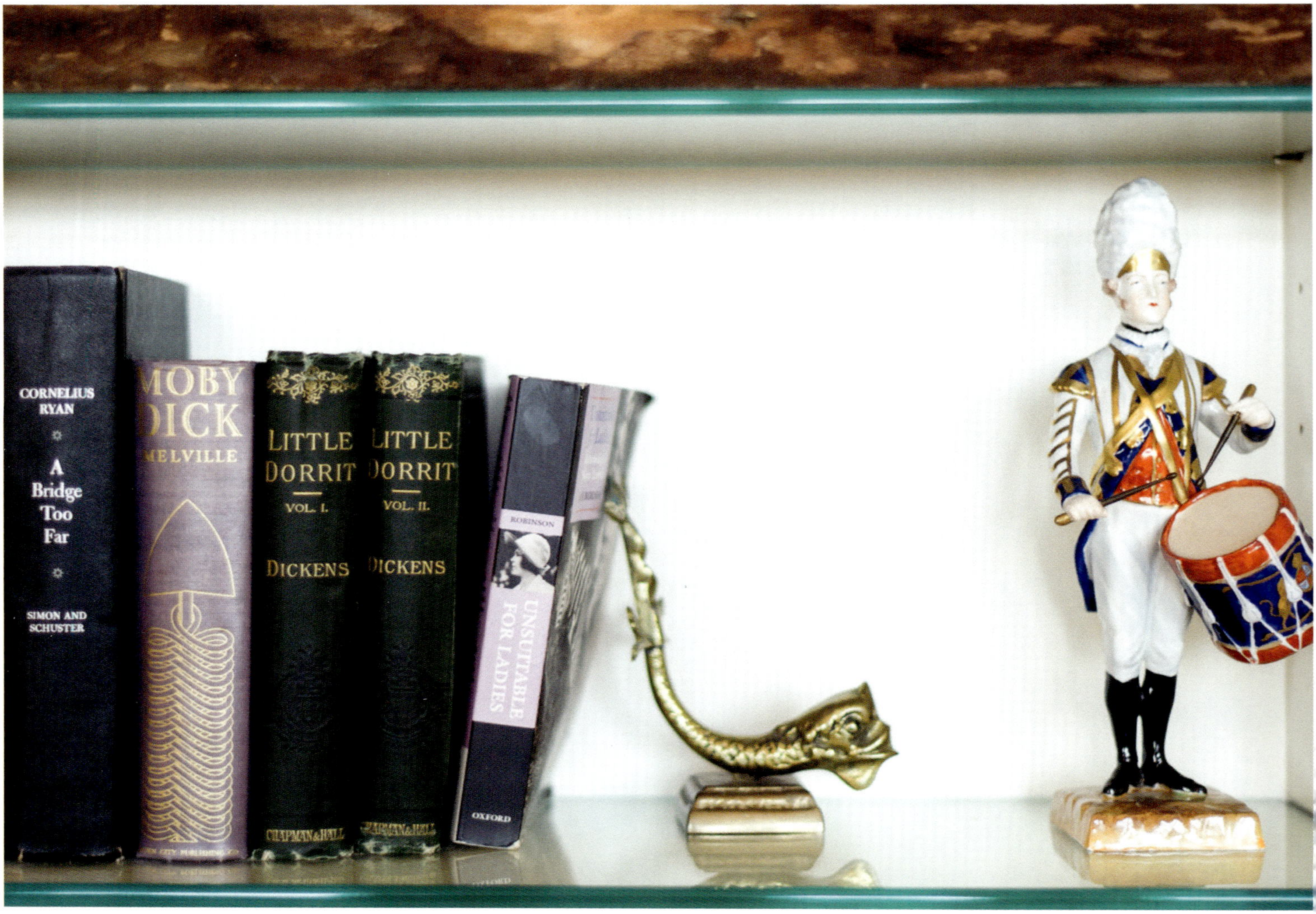
CORNELIUS RYAN
A Bridge Too Far
SIMON AND SCHUSTER
MOBY DICK
MELVILLE
LITTLE DORRIT
VOL. I.
DICKENS
CHAPMAN & HALL
LITTLE DORRIT
VOL. II.
DICKENS
ROBINSON
UNSUITABLE FOR LADIES
OXFORD

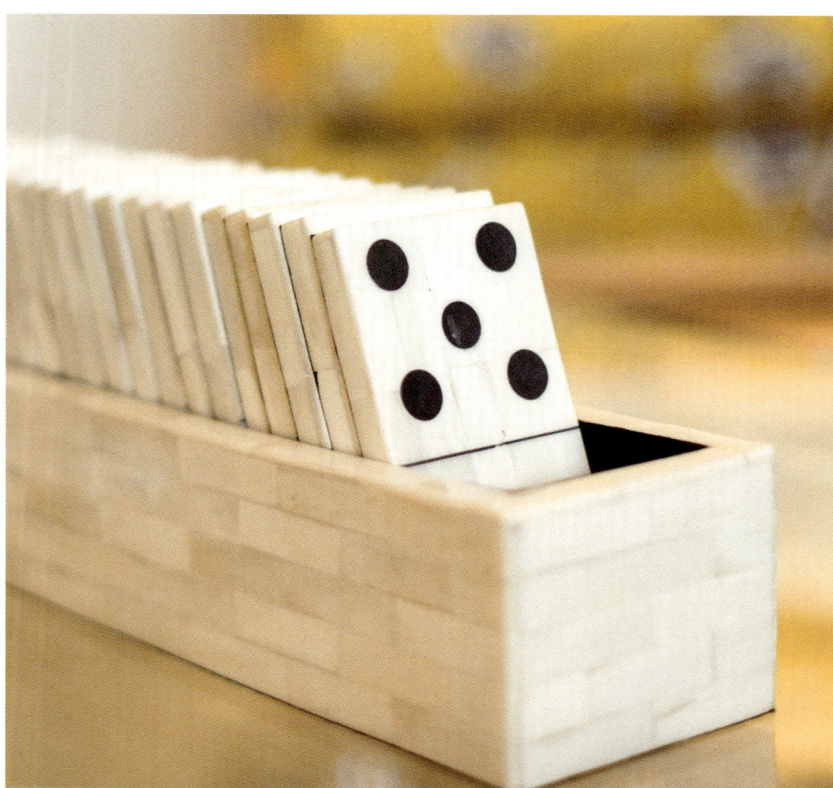

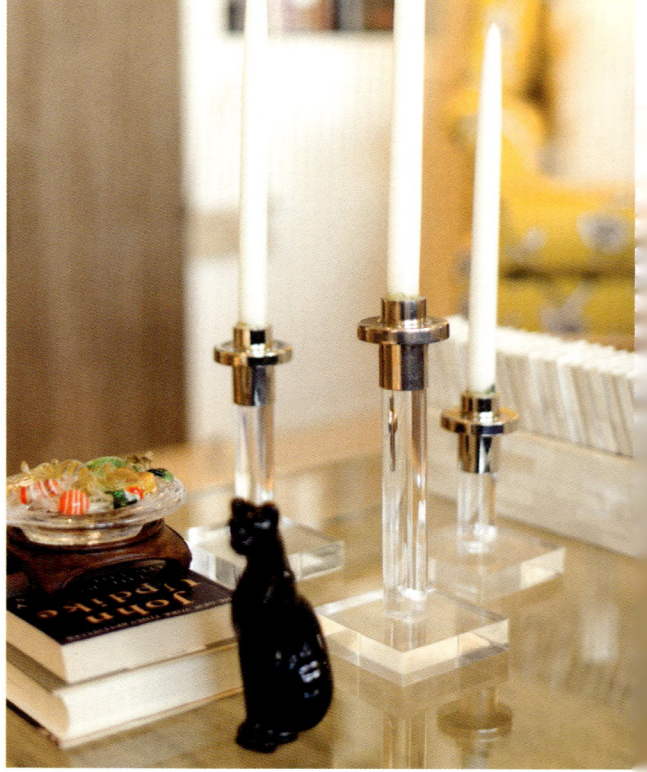

SARA'S TIPS
FOR
ARTFUL LIVING

Showing off my clients' various collections is my favorite decor tip. They're special because they're personal and almost always collected over time, which gives them a story. My suggestion is to group your collection together rather than spread it out over the house. The collection will have greater visual and emotional impact.

Gwenna is an amazing artist, so showcasing her work along with other pieces that are important to the family is a great way to adorn the walls in the entry and hallway. It not only makes a design statement when you first walk in, but more importantly, it says so much about this family.

The Pences inherited some great antiques, but like most antiques, they needed a little new life. To make them work in their home, we covered seats or entire pieces with updated fabrics to give these quality pieces a fresh feel.

Utilize pull out sofas. The artist corner has a pull out sofa perfect for overnight guests. This spot in particular is almost too great with the killer views – guests may never leave.

INSPIRED BY
tudor classic

TRADITIONAL RE-FRESH

THE THORNBERRY HOME

MEGAN THORNBERRY IS THE SIZE OF MY PINKY FINGER BUT HAS ENOUGH SPUNK IN HER TO FILL THREE OF ME. I LOVE HER ENERGY! REFERRED TO ME BY MOLLY MAXWELL, ANOTHER MUCH LOVED FRIEND AND CLIENT FEATURED IN THIS BOOK, I KNEW ANY FRIEND OF MOLLY'S WOULD BE A FRIEND OF MINE, AND I WASN'T WRONG. MEGAN IS A LAWYER, MOTHER OF TWO, ENTREPRENEUR, FRIEND, AND SO MUCH MORE.

Our work together began with her kids' rooms. These projects are the most fun for me but also the most terrifying. Kids don't fake it, so if they don't like something, they let you know. Their imaginations are big, so I work hard to create a space they will be excited about but that is grounded enough in reality that mom and dad will approve. Ellie and Topher's creativity and politeness stood out from the get-go. We created fun rooms that were approved by all.

Next, Megan and I tackled their main level. The living room and powder room got a large make over, although the bones were so good, it was purely cosmetic. It was a dramatic remodel, but the Thornberrys were the poor recipients of my first – and last – reveal. Who doesn't love the HGTV reveals? It's so exciting and fun. Yeah, well I learned my lesson the hard way, but thankfully with good people. For starters, it is a ton of work to complete a large project while the clients are away on vacation for a week. Lesson one: I didn't plan enough time. Lesson 2: there should be a party there waiting for them. Our reveal was just me waiting for the family to come home from vacation. A good idea, but I'm not really a jumping jack, hugging, yelling kind of girl, so it wasn't quite a moment made for movies. Although as usual, the family was gracious and appreciative, which was a joy.

We then moved to the master bedroom and the kids' bathroom. It's been a fun journey working our way through this cute Tudor home, and always, one of the best parts is the time I get to spend with Megan. An excellent business woman in her own right, she has become a mentor to me, always willing to talk about my business and give me great advice. It is one of the greatest pleasures in my work to form friendships with clients that last long after the remodeling is completed, and THAT is what makes the Thornberrys truly fabulous.

SARA'S TIPS
FOR
TRADITIONAL RE-FRESH

Wallpaper, wallpaper, wallpaper. A large print instantly decorates everything.

Navy is a neutral. If you are not doing an all neutral palette, then injecting color is necessary. Navy is a safe way to add color that isn't overwhelming and goes with almost anything. There's a reason a Brooks Brothers' navy suit is classic.

In a kid's room, mix up the colors. Bold is good. It may not be a color combo you would at first choose, but adding some unexpected color your kid loves keeps it fun.

Update your lighting and do not forget the sconces. Even simple updated sconces in the right finish will give a space an elevated feel. Sometimes the smallest fixes can add big impact.

MY TOUGHEST CLIENT

MY HOME

AS ANY DESIGNER I HAVE PLENTY OF STORIES ABOUT HIGH MAINTENANCE CLIENTS. BUT IT ALWAYS SURPRISES ME WHEN IT'S ME! AFTER MY DIVORCE AND A YEAR IN AN APARTMENT, THAT WAS A GREAT TIME FOR ME TO REGROUP, I GOT TO BUILD MY CURRENT HOME.

I look back and my life was spinning during those years. It was such a blessing that I got to build this home. It gave me a project that made me so happy. It gave me such satisfaction to do this for the kids. And while I like the freedom of apartment living the kids were ready for more space.

There were so many angels along the way for me. Chris George Custom Homes was the perfect builder for me. They gave me freedom to create my vision and help me do it on my tight budget. I told Chris I want a traditional exterior with a more modern inside and that's exactly what we did.

Vince entertained me and went with me most every night to check progress. I'm guessing he didn't want to talk about this project all the time but he not only humored me but encouraged me to create something I would be proud of. The house was elongated slightly to make sure we had room for a baby grand piano so Vince could play and I could accompany with my tambourine. A skill I don't share enough with others or my kids might tell you I share too much.

The sleek marble fireplace, the Kohler Karbon faucet that is functioned with a joystick, and the wallpaper in the kitchen are a few of my favorite fabulous takes on this house.

Building this home was an important milestone. It marked the beginning of our new normal and my desire to live my life out of a place of positivity and class. Everywhere I look, I see evidence of my taste, my style, my choices, my touch as well as the love that went into making this house a home. Far more important to me than the wallpaper or the light fixtures are the people inside this home that make everything worthwhile. Is this my forever home? No, I am sure it is not. It is one stop on this crazy, surprising, unpredictable journey. Who knows where it will lead next? Maybe a downtown loft? Perhaps a condo in Paris? I don't know, but one thing is for sure. Whatever it is, it's going to be nothing short of FABULOUS!

SARA'S TIPS
FOR
MY TOUGHEST CLIENT

Wallpaper an accent wall. Heck, wallpaper a couple. It's one of the most dramatic things you can do to a space. We often hear people say they want timeless, but I'm here to say that changing out wallpaper after ten years is not a big deal.

If you like lots of things, like I do, start with a boring canvas. My white walls and cabinetry are a great backdrop to my gallery of art.

Also, no need to scare from a white sofa anymore. Sunbrella and many others have saved the day so you can fearlessly have white furniture.

Buy a cheap rug for under the kitchen table. It hides messes better than your wood floor, it's easy to vacuum, and it adds warmth and texture to a space that usually doesn't have much of that.

Paint the trim and walls the same color for a dramatic look. It's just paint. You can change it if you tire of it in ten years.